Marking Classified National Security Information

As required by
Executive Order 13526, Classified National Security Information,
December 29, 2009, and
32 CFR Part 2001, ISOO Implementing Directive, effective June 25, 2010

December 2010
Revision 2, January 2014

Table of Contents

Introduction   2
Reminders   2

SECTION 1 – Originally Classified Documents   **3**
    Portion Marking   5
    Overall Classification Marking   6
    Classification Authority Block
        "Classified By" line   7
        "Reason" for classification line   8
        "Declassify On" line   9

SECTION 2 – Derivatively Classified Documents   **11**
    Portion Marking   12
    Overall Classification Marking   13
    Classification Authority Block
        "Classified By" line   14
        "Derived From" line   15
        "Declassify On" line   17
    Declassification Instructions
        Missing Declassification Instruction   18
        Multiple Sources   19
        OADR   21
        X1, X2, X3, X4, X5, X6, X7, and X8   22
        MR   23
        DNI Only/DCI Only   24
        Subject to Treaty or International Agreement   25
        25X1-human Exemption   26
        Use of 25X1 through 25X9 Exemptions   27
    Derivatively Classifying from a Classification Guide   28

SECTION 3 – Additional or Special Markings   **31**
    Classification Extensions   31
    Classification by Compilation   32
    Foreign Government Information   34
    Commingling RD and FRD with Information Classified under the Order   35
    Transmittal Document   36

SECTION 4 – Examples   **39**

SECTION 5 – Quick Reference   **47**

Summary of Changes   **51**

Introduction

Executive Order (E.O.) 13526 and its implementing directive, 32 CFR Part 2001, prescribe a uniform security classification system. This system requires that standard markings be applied to classified information. Except in extraordinary circumstances, or as approved by the Director of the Information Security Oversight Office (ISOO), the marking of classified information shall not deviate from the prescribed formats. Markings shall be uniformly and conspicuously applied to leave no doubt about the classified status of the information, the level of protection required, and the duration of classification. Since a booklet of this size cannot illustrate every conceivable situation, please refer to the implementing directive, other ISOO issuances, and any instructions issued by your organization for further clarification. Consult your security manager if you have any questions.

This booklet is unclassified, and as it is in the public domain, it may be reproduced without permission. All classification markings used are for illustration purposes only. All previous booklets and the guidance contained in them are rescinded.

Reminders

❖ Only individuals specifically authorized in writing may classify documents originally.

❖ Only individuals with the appropriate security clearance, who are required by their work to restate classified source information, may derivatively classify information.

❖ **Markings other than "Top Secret," "Secret," and "Confidential" shall not be used to identify classified national security information.**

❖ Information shall not be classified for any reason unrelated to the protection of the national security.

❖ Classifiers and authorized holders are responsible for ensuring that information is appropriately classified and properly marked.

❖ Individuals who believe that information in their possession is inappropriately classified, or inappropriately unclassified, are expected to bring their concerns to the attention of responsible officials.

❖ The following markings are not authorized in the "Declassify On" line:
  - "Originating Agency's Determination Required" or "OADR" for documents created after October 14, 1995;
  - "X1," "X2," "X3," "X4," "X5," "X6," "X7," or "X8" for documents created after September 22, 2003;
  - "Manual Review" or "MR;"
  - "DNI Only" or "DCI Only;"
  - "Subject to treaty or international agreement;" and
  - "25X1-human."

Section 1: Originally Classified Documents

The following is an example of a document that an original classifier has determined requires protection under E.O. 13526. It contains the primary markings required under the Order, including:

❖ Portion markings;

❖ Overall classification markings; and

❖ Classification authority block consisting of:

> • A "Classified By" line to include the identity, by name and position, or by personal identifier of the original classifier, and if not otherwise evident, the agency and office of origin.
>
> • The "Reason" for classification as provided in section 1.4 of the Order.
>
> • A "Declassify On" line which shall indicate one of the following durations of classification:
>
> > ✓ A date or event for declassification that corresponds to the lapse of the information's national security sensitivity, which is equal to or less than 10 years from the date of the original decision.
> >
> > ✓ A date not to exceed 25 years from the date of the original decision.
> >
> > ✓ If the classified information should clearly and demonstrably be expected to reveal the identity of a confidential human source or a human intelligence source, no date or event shall be annotated and the marking "50X1-HUM" shall be used.
> >
> > ✓ If the classified information should clearly and demonstrably be expected to reveal key design concepts of weapons of mass destruction, no date or event shall be annotated and the marking "50X2-WMD" shall be used.

NOTE: Ensure the document you create is dated. Having the correct date of origin of the document may be critical when creating other documents using your originally classified document as a source.

Department of Good Works
Washington, D.C. 20006

June 27, 2010

MEMORANDUM FOR THE DIRECTOR

From: John E. Doe, Chief Division 5

Subject: Examples

1. Paragraph 1 contains "Unclassified" information. Therefore, this portion will be marked with the designation "U" in parentheses preceding the portion.

2. Paragraph 2 contains "Secret" information. Therefore, this portion will be marked with the designation "S" in parentheses preceding the portion.

3. Paragraph 3 contains "Confidential" information. Therefore, this portion will be marked with the designation "C" in parentheses preceding the portion.

> **Document before the markings are applied.**

> **Document after the markings are applied.**

SECRET

 Department of Good Works
Washington, D.C. 20006

June 27, 2010

MEMORANDUM FOR THE DIRECTOR

From: John E. Doe, Chief Division 5

Subject: (U) Examples

1. (U) Paragraph 1 contains "Unclassified" information. Therefore, this portion will be marked with the designation "U" in parentheses preceding the portion.

2. (S) Paragraph 2 contains "Secret" information. Therefore, this portion will be marked with the designation "S" in parentheses preceding the portion.

3. (C) Paragraph 3 contains "Confidential" information. Therefore, this portion will be marked with the designation "C" in parentheses preceding the portion.

Classified By: John E. Doe, Chief Division 5
Reason: 1.4(a)
Declassify On: 20150627

SECRET

> *NOTE: The date for declassification may be displayed either by spelling out the month (June 27, 2015), or numerically (20150627). When displayed numerically, the following format must be used: YYYYMMDD.*

Step 1 – Portion marking

❖ Identify the classification level of each portion.

- A portion is ordinarily defined as a paragraph, but also includes subjects, titles, graphics, tables, charts, bullet statements, sub-paragraphs, classified signature blocks, bullets and other portions within slide presentations, and the like.
- Portion markings consist of the letters "(U)" for Unclassified, "(C)" for Confidential, "(S)" for Secret, and "(TS)" for Top Secret.
- The two paragraphs of this sample document contain "Secret" and "Unclassified" information, respectively.
- The abbreviations, in parentheses, are placed before the portion to which they apply. Portion mark as illustrated in this example.

 Department of Good Works
Washington, D.C. 20006

June 27, 2010

MEMORANDUM FOR THE DIRECTOR

From: John E. Doe, Chief Division 5

Subject: (U) Examples

1. (U) Paragraph 1 contains "Unclassified" information. Therefore, this portion will be marked with the designation "U" in parentheses preceding the portion.

   - (S) If all sub-paragraphs are the same classification as the primary paragraph, then you do not need to portion mark the sub-paragraphs.

   - (U) However, if the portions are not all the same classification, then all main and sub-paragraphs must be individually marked.

2. (S) Paragraph 2 contains "Secret" information. Therefore, this portion will be marked with the designation "S" in parentheses preceding the portion.

NOTE: *Portion marking waivers may be requested by an agency head or senior agency official. Such requests shall be submitted to the Director of ISOO. See 32 CFR Part 2001.24(k) for more information.*

Step 2 – Overall classification marking

❖ Identify the overall classification of the document. This will be equal to the highest classification level of any one portion found in the document. In this example, the highest classification is "Secret," found in paragraph 2.

- Conspicuously place the overall classification at the top and bottom of the page.
- If the document contains more than one page, place the overall marking at the top and bottom of the outside of the front cover, on the title page, on the first page, and on the outside of the back cover (if any).
- Mark other internal pages either with the overall classification or with a marking indicating the highest classification level of information contained on that page.

SECRET

 Department of Good Works
Washington, D.C. 20006

June 27, 2010

MEMORANDUM FOR THE DIRECTOR

From: John E. Doe, Chief Division 5

Subject: (U) Examples

1. (U) Paragraph 1 contains "Unclassified" information. Therefore, this portion will be marked with the designation "U" in parentheses preceding the portion.

2. (S) Paragraph 2 contains "Secret" information. Therefore, this portion will be marked with the designation "S" in parentheses preceding the portion.

3. (C) Paragraph 3 contains "Confidential" information. Therefore, this portion will be marked with the designation "C" in parentheses preceding the portion.

SECRET

NOTE: Some agencies require additional dissemination and control markings that accompany the overall classification markings. Contact your security manager for agency-specific guidelines.

Step 3 – Classification authority block: "Classified By" line

❖ Identify the original classification authority (OCA) by <u>name and position</u> or <u>personal identifier.</u>
  • If the identity of the originating agency or office is not apparent on the face of the document, place it immediately following the name and position or personal identifier provided in the "Classified By" line.

SECRET

Department of Good Works
Washington, D.C. 20006

June 27, 2010

MEMORANDUM FOR THE DIRECTOR

From: John E. Doe, Chief Division 5

Subject: (U) Examples

1. (U) Paragraph 1 contains "Unclassified" information. Therefore, this portion will be marked with the designation "U" in parentheses preceding the portion.

2. (S) Paragraph 2 contains "Secret" information. Therefore, this portion will be marked with the designation "S" in parentheses preceding the portion.

3. (C) Paragraph 3 contains "Confidential" information. Therefore, this portion will be marked with the designation "C" in parentheses preceding the portion.

Classified By: John E. Doe, Chief Division 5

SECRET

OCA by name and position

SECRET

Department of Good Works
Washington, D.C. 20006

June 27, 2010

MEMORANDUM FOR THE DIRECTOR

From: John E. Doe, Chief Division 5

Subject: (U) Examples

1. (U) Paragraph 1 contains "Unclassified" information. Therefore, this portion will be marked with the designation "U" in parentheses preceding the portion.

2. (S) Paragraph 2 contains "Secret" information. Therefore, this portion will be marked with the designation "S" in parentheses preceding the portion.

3. (C) Paragraph 3 contains "Confidential" information. Therefore, this portion will be marked with the designation "C" in parentheses preceding the portion.

Classified By: ID # 54632

SECRET

OCA by personal identifier

Step 4 – Classification authority block: "Reason" for classification line

❖ Place the number 1.4 plus the letter(s) that correspond(s) to the classification category in section 1.4 of E.O. 13526. These categories, as they appear in the Order, include the following:

(a) military plans, weapons systems, or operations;

(b) foreign government information;

(c) intelligence activities (including covert action), intelligence sources or methods, or cryptology;

(d) foreign relations or foreign activities of the United States, including confidential sources;

(e) scientific, technological, or economic matters relating to the national security;

(f) United States Government programs for safeguarding nuclear materials or facilities;

(g) vulnerabilities or capabilities of systems, installations, infrastructures, projects, plans, or protection services relating to the national security; or

(h) the development, production, or use of weapons of mass destruction.

SECRET

Department of Good Works
Washington, D.C. 20006

June 27, 2010

MEMORANDUM FOR THE DIRECTOR

From: John E. Doe, Chief Division 5

Subject: (U) Examples

1. (U) Paragraph 1 contains "Unclassified" information. Therefore, this portion will be marked with the designation "U" in parentheses preceding the portion.

2. (S) Paragraph 2 contains "Secret" information. Therefore, this portion will be marked with the designation "S" in parentheses preceding the portion.

3. (C) Paragraph 3 contains "Confidential" information. Therefore, this portion will be marked with the designation "C" in parentheses preceding the portion.

Classified By: John E. Doe, Chief Division 5
Reason: 1.4(c)

SECRET

Step 5 – Classification authority block: "Declassify On" line

❖ This indicates the duration of classification. An original classifier must choose one of the following declassification instructions, selecting whenever possible, the declassification instruction that will result in the shortest duration of classification.

✓ A date or event that is less than 10 years from the date of original classification (date of document is July 1, 2010)

> Classified By: John E. Doe, Chief Division 5
> Reason: 1.4(a)
> Declassify On: 20150701

✓ A date that is 10 years from the date of the original classification decision (date of document is July 1, 2010)

> Classified By: John E. Doe, Chief Division 5
> Reason: 1.4(a)
> Declassify On: 20200701

✓ A date not to exceed 25 years from the date of the original classification decision (date of document is July 1, 2010).

> Classified By: John E. Doe, Chief Division 5
> Reason: 1.4(a)
> Declassify On: 20350701

❖ Exceptions to this sequence:

✓ If the information should clearly and demonstrably be expected to reveal the identity of a confidential human source or a human intelligence source, the duration of classification shall be up to 75 years and shall be designated as 50X1-HUM.

> Classified By: John E. Doe, Chief Division 5
> Reason: 1.4(c)
> Declassify On: 50X1-HUM

✓ If the information should clearly and demonstrably be expected to reveal key design concepts of weapons of mass destruction, the duration shall be up to 75 years and shall be designated as 50X2-WMD.

> Classified By: John E. Doe, Chief Division 5
> Reason: 1.4(h)
> Declassify On: 50X2-WMD

> *NOTE: When __50X1-HUM__ and __50X2-WMD__ are used, a specific date or event for declassification of the information will not be used. Approval by the ISCAP is not required prior to agency use of 50X1-HUM or 50X2-WMD; however, it will need to be included in a classification guide with sufficient detail to enable effective use.*

Section 2: Derivatively Classified Documents

Derivative classification is the act of incorporating, paraphrasing, restating, or generating in new form information that is already classified, and marking the newly developed material consistent with the markings of the source information. The source information ordinarily consists of a classified document or documents, or a classification guide issued by an original classification authority.

When using a classified source document as the basis for derivative classification, the markings on the source document determine the markings to be applied to the derivative document. When using a classification guide as the basis for derivative classification, the instructions provided by the guide are to be applied to the derivative document.

The following examples are of a properly marked source document and a properly marked derivative document, followed by the steps taken to create the derivative document.

Source Document

SECRET

Department of Good Works
Washington, D.C. 20006

June 27, 2010

MEMORANDUM FOR THE DIRECTOR

From: John E. Doe, Chief Division 5

Subject: (U) Examples

1. (U) Paragraph 1 contains unclassified information. Therefore, this portion will be marked with the designation "U" in parentheses preceding the portion.

2. (S) Paragraph 2 contains "Secret" information. Therefore, this portion will be marked with the designation "S" in parentheses preceding the portion.

3. (C) Paragraph 3 contains "Confidential" information. Therefore, this portion will be marked with the designation "C" in parentheses preceding the portion.

Classified By: John E. Doe, Chief Division 5
Reason: 1.4(a)
Declassify On: 20151231

SECRET

Derivative Document

SECRET

Department of Information
Washington, D.C. 20008

July 15, 2010

MEMORANDUM FOR AGENCY OFFICIALS

From: Joe Carver, Director

Subject: (U) Examples

1. (S) Paragraph 1 contains information from Paragraph 2 in the source document and is therefore marked (S).

2. (U) Paragraph 2 contains "Unclassified" information. Therefore, this portion will be marked with the designation "U" in parentheses preceding the portion.

Classified By: Joe Carver, Director
Derived From: Department of Good Works Memorandum dated June 27, 2010, Subj: (U) Examples
Declassify On: 20151231

SECRET

Source Document

SECRET

Department of Good Works
Washington, D.C. 20006

June 27, 2010

MEMORANDUM FOR THE DIRECTOR

From: John E. Doe, Chief Division 5

Subject: (U) Examples

1. (U) Paragraph 1 contains "Unclassified" information. Therefore, this portion will be marked with the designation "U" in parentheses preceding the portion.

2. (S) Paragraph 2 contains "Secret" information. Therefore, this portion will be marked with the designation "S" in parentheses preceding the portion.

3. (C) Paragraph 3 contains "Confidential" information. Therefore, this portion will be marked with the designation "C" in parentheses preceding the portion.

Classified By: John E. Doe, Chief Division 5
Reason: 1.4(a)
Declassify On: 20151231

SECRET

Step 1 - Portion marking

Paragraph 1 of the derivative document incorporates information from paragraph 2 of the source document. Therefore, the portion marking is carried over to the derivative document.

Derivative Document

Department of Information
Washington, D.C. 20008

July 15, 2010

MEMORANDUM FOR AGENCY OFFICIALS

From: Joe Carver, Director

Subject: (U) Examples

1. (S) Paragraph 1 contains information from Paragraph 2 in the source document and is therefore marked (S).

2. (U) Paragraph 2 contains "Unclassified" information. Therefore, this portion will be marked with the designation "U" in parentheses preceding the portion.

Source Document

SECRET

Department of Good Works
Washington, D.C. 20006

June 27, 2010

MEMORANDUM FOR THE DIRECTOR

From: John E. Doe, Chief Division 5

Subject: (U) Examples

1. (U) Paragraph 1 contains "Unclassified" information. Therefore, this portion will be marked with the designation "U" in parentheses preceding the portion.

2. (S) Paragraph 2 contains "Secret" information. Therefore, this portion will be marked with the designation "S" in parentheses preceding the portion.

3. (C) Paragraph 3 contains "Confidential" informat[ion] Therefore, this portion will be marked with the designation "C" in parentheses preceding the portio[n]

Classified By: John E. Doe, Chief Division 5
Reason: 1.4(a)
Declassify On: 20151231

SECRET

Step 2 - Overall classification marking

The highest level of any portion of this derivative document is "Secret." Therefore, conspicuously place an overall classification of "SECRET" at the top and bottom of the derivative document.

Derivative Document

SECRET

Department of Information
Washington, D.C. 20008

July 15, 2010

MEMORANDUM FOR AGENCY OFFICIALS

From: Joe Carver, Director

Subject: (U) Examples

1. (S) Paragraph 1 contains information from Paragraph 2 in the source document and is therefore marked (S).

2. (U) Paragraph 2 contains "Unclassified" information. Therefore, this portion will be marked with the designation "U" in parentheses preceding the portion.

SECRET

Source Document

SECRET

Department of Good Works
Washington, D.C. 20006

June 27, 2010

MEMORANDUM FOR THE DIRECTOR

From: John E. Doe, Chief Division 5

Subject: (U) Examples

1. (U) Paragraph 1 contains "Unclassified" information. Therefore, this portion will be marked with the designation "U" in parentheses preceding the portion.

2. (S) Paragraph 2 contains "Secret" information. Therefore, this portion will be marked with the designation "S" in parentheses preceding the portion.

3. (C) Paragraph 3 contains "Confidential" inform[...] Therefore, this portion will be marked with the designation "C" in parentheses preceding the port[...]

Classified By: John E. Doe, Chief Division 5
Reason: 1.4(a)
Declassify On: 20151231

SECRET

Step 3 – Classification authority block: "Classified By" line

Derivative classifiers shall be identified by <u>name and position</u>, or by <u>personal identifier</u>, in a manner that is immediately apparent on each derivatively classified document.

Derivative Document

SECRET

Department of Information
Washington, D.C. 20008

July 15, 2010

MEMORANDUM FOR AGENCY OFFICIALS

From: Joe Carver, Director

Subject: (U) Examples

1. (S) Paragraph 1 contains information from Paragraph 2 in the source document and is therefore marked (S).

2. (U) Paragraph 2 contains "Unclassified" information. Therefore, this portion will be marked with the designation "U" in parentheses preceding the portion.

Classified By: Joe Carver, Director

SECRET

NOTE: If not otherwise evident, the agency and office of origin shall be identified and placed immediately following the name and position or personal identifier provided in the "Classified By" line.

Source Document

SECRET

Department of Good Works
Washington, D.C. 20006

June 27, 2010

MEMORANDUM FOR THE DIRECTOR

From: John E. Doe, Chief Division 5

Subject: (U) Examples

1. (U) Paragraph 1 contains "Unclassified" information. Therefore, this portion will be marked with the designation "U" in parentheses preceding the portion.

2. (S) Paragraph 2 contains "Secret" information. Therefore, this portion will be marked with the designation "S" in parentheses preceding the portion.

3. (C) Paragraph 3 contains "Confidential" information. Therefore, this portion will be marked with the designation "C" in parentheses preceding the portion.

Step 4 – Classification authority block: "Derived From" line

Precisely identify the source document or the classification guide on the "Derived From" line, including the agency and, where available, the office of origin, and the date of the source or guide.

Derivative Document

SECRET

Department of Information
Washington, D.C. 20008

July 15, 2010

MEMORANDUM FOR AGENCY OFFICIALS

From: Joe Carver, Director

Subject: (U) Examples

1. (S) Paragraph 1 contains information from Paragraph 2 in the source document and is therefore marked (S).

2. (U) Paragraph 2 contains "Unclassified" information. Therefore, this portion will be marked with the designation "U" in parentheses preceding the portion.

Classified By: Joe Carver, Director
Derived From: Department of Good Works
Memorandum dated June 27, 2010, Subj: (U) Examples

SECRET

Step 4 - "Derived From" line, cont'd

When using multiple source documents, the "Derived From" line shall appear as:

Derived From: Multiple Sources

The derivative classifier shall include a listing of the source materials on, or attached to, each derivatively classified document. There is no required placement of the source list within the document, only that it be included in, or attached to, the document.

Example

Example

> Sources:
>
> 1. **Dept of Good Works Memorandum dated June 27, 2010, Subj: Examples**
> 2. **Dept of Good Works Memorandum dated May 30, 2009, Subj: Examples**
> 3. **Radar SCG dated February 2, 2006, Section 12, item 7.**

A document derivatively classified on the basis of a source document that is itself marked "Multiple Sources" shall cite the source document on its "Derived From" line rather than the term "Multiple Sources." An example might appear as:

Source Document

SECRET

 Department of Good Works
Washington, D.C. 20006

June 27, 2010

MEMORANDUM FOR THE DIRECTOR

From: John E. Doe, Chief Division 5

Subject: (U) Examples

1. (U) Paragraph 1 contains "Unclassified" information. Therefore, this portion will be marked with the designation "U" in parentheses preceding the portion.

2. (S) Paragraph 2 contains "Secret" information. Therefore, this portion will be marked with the designation "S" in parentheses preceding the portion.

Classified By: John E. Doe, Chief Division 5
Derived From: Multiple Sources
Declassify On: 20200627

SECRET

Derivative Document

SECRET

 Department of Information
Washington, D.C. 20008

July 15, 2010

MEMORANDUM FOR AGENCY OFFICIALS

From: Joe Carver, Director

Subject: (U) Examples

1. (S) Paragraph 1 contains information from Paragraph 2 in the source document and is therefore marked (S).

2. (U) Paragraph 2 contains "Unclassified" information. Therefore, this portion will be marked with the designation "U" in parentheses preceding the portion.

Classified By: Joe Carver, Director
Derived From: Department of Good Works Memorandum dated June 27, 2010, Subj: Examples
Declassify On: 20200627

SECRET

Source Document

SECRET

Department of Good Works
Washington, D.C. 20006

June 27, 2010

MEMORANDUM FOR THE DIRECTOR

From: John E. Doe, Chief Division 5

Subject: (U) Examples

1. (U) Paragraph 1 contains "Unclassified" information. Therefore, this portion will be marked with the designation "U" in parentheses preceding the portion.

2. (S) Paragraph 2 contains "Secret" information. Therefore, this portion will be marked with the designation "S" in parentheses preceding the portion.

3. (C) Paragraph 3 contains "Confidential" informa[tion]. Therefore, this portion will be marked with the designation "C" in parentheses preceding the portio[n].

Classified By: John E. Doe, Chief Division 5
Reason: 1.4(a)
Declassify On 20150627

SECRET

Step 5 – Classification authority block: "Declassify On" line

The derivative classifier shall carry forward the instructions on the "Declassify On" line from the source document to the derivative document, or the duration instruction from the classification or declassification guide. *(See the following pages for additional guidance when the source document contains missing, unauthorized, or multiple declassification instructions.)*

Derivative Document

SECRET

Department of Information
Washington, D.C. 20008

July 15, 2010

MEMORANDUM FOR AGENCY OFFICIALS

From: Joe Carver, Director

Subject: (U) Examples

1. (S) Paragraph 1 contains information from Paragraph 2 in the source document and is therefore marked (S).

2. (U) Paragraph 2 contains "Unclassified" information. Therefore, this portion will be marked with the designation "U" in parentheses preceding the portion.

Classified By: Joe Carver, Director
Derived From: Department of Good Works Memorandum dated June 27, 2010, Subj: (U) Examples
Declassify On: 20150627

SECRET

Declassification Instructions on Derivatively Classified Documents:

If the source document is missing the declassification instruction, then a calculated date of 25 years from the date of the source document (if available) or the current date (if the source document date is not available) shall be carried forward by the derivative classifier.

Source Document

Missing declassification instruction

SECRET

 Department of Good Works
Washington, D.C. 20006

June 27, 2010

MEMORANDUM FOR THE DIRECTOR

From: John E. Doe, Chief Division 5

Subject: (U) Examples

1. (U) Paragraph 1 contains "Unclassified" information. Therefore, this portion will be marked with the designation "U" in parentheses.

2. (S) Paragraph 2 contains "Secret" information. Therefore, this portion will be marked with the designation "S" in parentheses.

3. (C) Paragraph 3 contains "Confidential" information. Therefore, this portion will be marked with the designation "C" in parentheses.

Classified By: John E. Doe, Chief Division 5
Reason: 1.4(a)

SECRET

Derivative Document

Classified By: Joe Carver, Director
Derived From: Department of Good Works
Memorandum dated June 27, 2010, Subj: (U) Examples
Declassify on: 20350627

SECRET

Section 2: Derivatively Classified Documents

Declassification Instructions on Derivatively Classified Documents:

When a document is classified derivatively on the basis of more than one source document or more than one element of a classification guide, the "Declassify On" line shall reflect the longest duration of classification of any of its sources.

Source Document 1

SECRET

Department of Good Works
Washington, D.C. 20006

June 27, 2010

MEMORANDUM FOR THE DIRECTOR

From: John E. Doe, Chief Division 5

Subject: (U) Examples

1. (U) Paragraph 1 contains "Unclassified" information. Therefore, this portion will be marked with the designation "U" in parentheses preceding the portion.

2. (S) Paragraph 2 contains "Secret" information. Therefore, this portion will be marked with the designation "S" in parentheses preceding the portion.

Classified By: John E. Doe, Chief Division 5
Reason: 1.4(a)
Declassify On: 20151231

SECRET

Source Document 2

SECRET

Department of Good Works
Washington, D.C. 20006

MEMORANDUM FOR THE DIRECTOR

From: John E. Doe, Chief Division 5

Subject: (U) Examples

1. (U) Paragraph 1 contains "Unclassified" information. Therefore, this portion will be marked with the designation "U" in parentheses preceding the portion.

2. (S) Paragraph 2 contains "Secret" information. Therefore, this portion will be marked with the designation "S" in parentheses preceding the portion.

Classified By: John E. Doe, Chief Division 5
Reason: 1.4(a)
Declassify On: 20290530

SECRET

Of the two declassification dates, 20151231 and 20290530, the date from source document 2 has the longest duration of classification and will be carried forward to the derivative document.

Classified By: Joe Carver, Director
Derived From: Multiple Sources
Declassify On: 20290530

SECRET **Derivative Document**

If the source documents contain multiple 25X markings, only one of the markings is required to be placed on the derivative document, as long as it is the one with the longest duration of classification. For example:

Document 1 – 25X3, 20350215
Document 2 – 25X5, 20320510
Document 3 – 25X4, 20301220

The marking from document 1 (25X3, 20350215) would be carried over to the derivative document and placed in the "Declassify On" line.

When determining the most restrictive declassification instruction among multiple source documents for placement in the "Declassify On" line, adhere to the following hierarchy:

---

1. "50X1-HUM" or "50X2-WMD" exemptions, or an approved exemption ("50X1" through "50X9") reflecting the ISCAP approval for classification beyond 50 years in accordance with section 3.3(h)(2) of the Order.

2. "25X1" through "25X9" exemptions, with a date or event.

3. A specific declassification date or event within 25 years.

4. Absent guidance from an original classification authority with jurisdiction over the information, a calculated 25-year date from the date of the source document.

Reference: 32 CFR Part 2001.22(e)(4)

Declassification Instructions on Derivatively Classified Documents:

When a document is classified derivatively either from a source document(s) or a classification guide that contains one of the following obsolete declassification instructions, "Originating Agency's Determination Required," "OADR," or "Manual Review," "MR," or any of the exemption markings "X1, X2, X3, X4, X5, X6, X7, and X8," the derivative classifier shall calculate a date that is 25 years from the date of the source document when determining a derivative document's date or event to be placed in the "Declassify On" line.

Source Document

OADR

SECRET

Department of Good Works
Washington, D.C. 20006

February 2, 1994

MEMORANDUM FOR THE DIRECTOR

From: John E. Doe, Chief Division 5

Subject: (U) Examples

1. (U) Paragraph 1 contains "Unclassified" information. Therefore, this portion will be marked with the designation "U" in parentheses preceding the portion.

2. (S) Paragraph 2 contains "Secret" information. Therefore, this portion will be marked with the designation "S" in parentheses preceding the portion.

Classified By: John E. Doe, Chief Division 5
Reason: 1.4(a)
Declassify On: OADR

SECRET

NOTE: Executive Order 12958, issued in 1995, eliminated the use of "OADR" on documents created on or after October 14, 1995.

Derivative Document

Classified By: Joe Carver, Director
Derived From: Department of Good Works
             Memorandum dated Feb 2, 1994
             Subj: (U) Examples
Declassify On: 20190202

Do not carry forward "OADR."
Change "OADR" to 25 years from
the date of the source document

If the source document does not contain a date, then the declassification date on the derivative document will be 25 years from the date of the derivative document's creation.

Declassification Instructions on Derivatively Classified Documents:

When a document is classified derivatively either from a source document(s) or a classification guide that contains one of the following obsolete declassification instructions, "Originating Agency's Determination Required," "OADR," or "Manual Review," "MR," or any of the exemption markings "X1, X2, X3, X4, X5, X6, X7, and X8," the derivative classifier shall calculate a date that is 25 years from the date of the source document when determining a derivative document's date or event to be placed in the "Declassify On" line.

Source Document

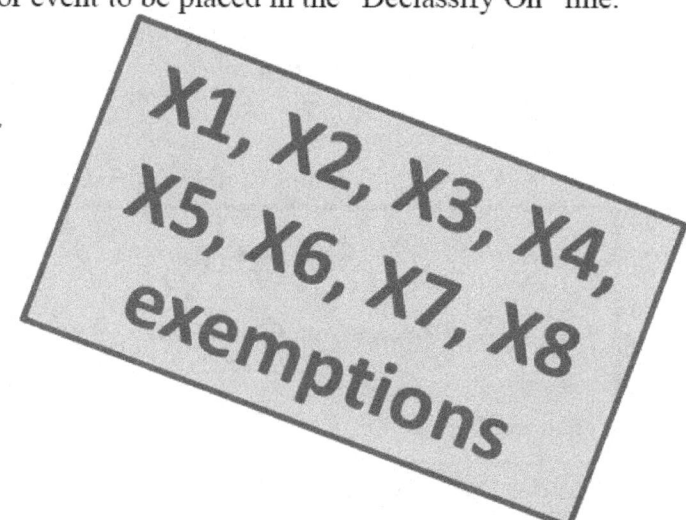

SECRET

 Department of Good Works
Washington, D.C. 20006

August 20, 2002

MEMORANDUM FOR THE DIRECTOR

From: John E. Doe, Chief Division 5

Subject: (U) Examples

1. (U) Paragraph 1 contains "Unclassified" information. Therefore, this portion will be marked with the designation "U" in parentheses preceding the portion.

2. (S) Paragraph 2 contains "Secret" information. Therefore, this portion will be marked with the designation "S" in parentheses preceding the portion.

3. (C) Paragraph 3 contains "Confidential" information. Therefore, this portion will be marked with the designation "C" in parentheses preceding the portion.

Classified By: John E. Doe, Chief Division 5
Reason: 1.4(a)
Declassify on: X3

SECRET

NOTE: Executive Order 12958, as amended, issued in 2003, eliminated the use of X1, X2, X3, X4, X5, X6, X7, and X8 on documents created on or after September 22, 2003.

Derivative Document

Classified By: Joe Carver, Director
Derived From: Department of Good Works Memorandum dated
   Aug 20, 2002, Subj: (U) Examples
Declassify On: 20270820

SECRET

Do not carry forward "X3."
Change "X3" to 25 years from the date of the source document

If the source document does not contain a date, then the declassification date on the derivative document will be 25 years from the date of the derivative document's creation.

Declassification Instructions on Derivatively Classified Documents:

When a document is classified derivatively either from a source document(s) or a classification guide that contains one of the following obsolete declassification instructions, "Originating Agency's Determination Required," "OADR," or "Manual Review," "MR," or any of the exemption markings X1, X2, X3, X4, X5, X6, X7, and X8, the derivative classifier shall calculate a date that is 25 years from the date of the source document when determining a derivative document's date or event to be placed in the "Declassify On" line.

Source Document

SECRET

Department of Good Works
Washington, D.C. 20006

February 15, 2004

MEMORANDUM FOR THE DIRECTOR

From: John E. Doe, Chief Division 5

Subject: (U) Examples

1. (U) Paragraph 1 contains "Unclassified" information. Therefore, this portion will be marked with the designation "U" in parentheses preceding the portion.

2. (S) Paragraph 2 contains "Secret" information. Therefore, this portion will be marked with the designation "S" in parentheses preceding the portion.

3. (C) Paragraph 3 contains "Confidential" information. Therefore, this portion will be marked with the designation "C" in parentheses preceding the portion.

Classified By: John E. Doe, Chief Division 5
Reason: 1.4(a)
Declassify On: MR

SECRET

MR

> *NOTE: "MR" (Manual Review) was neither intended nor authorized as a marking for the "Declassify on" line on documents classified under any executive order. If "MR" appears in the "Declassify on" line of a source document, mark the derivative document with a declassification date no more than 25 years from the date of the source document.*

Derivative Document

Classified By: Joan Smith, Program Analyst
Derived From: Department of Good Works Memorandum
dated Feb 15, 2004, Subj: (U) Examples
Declassify On: 20290215

SECRET

Do not carry forward "MR."
Change "MR" to 25 years from the date of the source document

If the source document does not contain a date, then the declassification date on the derivative document will be 25 years from the date of the derivative document's creation.

Declassification Instructions on Derivatively Classified Documents:

"DNI Only" and "DCI Only" are no longer valid declassification instructions and, if annotated on the source document, will not be carried over to the derivative document.

> *NOTE: E.O. 12951, Release of Imagery Acquired by Space-Based National Intelligence Reconnaissance Systems, gives the Director of National Intelligence (DNI) the authority to declassify intelligence imagery.*

If the document **contains imagery**, as described in E.O. 12951, the derivative classifier will mark the derivative document in the following manner: Declassify on: 25X1, E.O. 12951.

DNI Only and DCI Only

Source Document

> SECRET
> Department of Good Works
> Washington, D.C. 20006
>
> Xxxxxxxxxxxxxxxxxxxxxxxxxxxxxx
> Xxxxxxxxxxxxxxxxxxxxxxxxxxxxxx
>
>
>
> Classified By: OCA name and position
> Reason: 1.4(a)
> Declassify On: DCI Only
>
> SECRET

Derivative Document

> SECRET
> Department of Good Works
> Washington, D.C. 20006
>
> Xxxxxxxxxxxxxxxxxxxxxxxxxxxxxxxxxxxxx
> xxxxxxxxxxxxxxxxxxxxxxxxxxxx.
>
>
>
> Classified By: Derivative classifier's name
> Derived From: Dept of Good Works Memo,
>   dtd July 15, 2010
> Declassify On: 25X1, E.O. 12951
>
> SECRET

If **no imagery** is carried forward to the derivative document, a declassification date will be calculated 25 years from the date of the source document.

Source Document

> July 15, 2010
>
> Xxxxxxxxxxxxxxxxxxxxxx
> xxxxxxxxxxxxxxxxxxxxxx
> xxxxxx.
>
> Classified By: OCA
> Reason: 1.4(a)
> Declassify On: DNI Only

Derivative Document

> January 21, 2011
>
> Xxxxxxxxxxxxxxxxxxxxxxxxxxxx
> xxxxxxxxxxx.
>
> Classified By: derivative
>   classifier's name
> Derived From: Dept of Good
>   Works Memo, dtd July 15, 2010
> Declassify On: 20350715

Declassification Instructions on Derivatively Classified Documents:

When creating a new, originally classified U.S. document containing FGI, the statement "Subject to Treaty or International Agreement" is not to be used in the "Declassify On" line.

Classified By: John E. Doe, Chief Division 5
Derived From: Multiple Sources
Declassify On: Subject to Treaty or International Agreement

SECRET

THIS DOCUMENT CONTAINS (COUNTRY
OF ORIGIN) INFORMATION

> *NOTE: Additional guidance on marking documents containing FGI can be found on page 32.*

If this marking still appears on a document being used as a source, the marking annotated on the derivative document will be changed to a date that is 25 years from the date of the source document. If the source document does not contain a date, then the declassification date will be 25 years from the date of the derivative document's creation.

Source Document

May 15, 2000

Classified By: John E. Doe, Chief Division 5
Derived From: Multiple Sources
Declassify On: Subject to Treaty or International
  Agreement

SECRET

THIS DOCUMENT CONTAINS (COUNTRY
OF ORIGIN) INFORMATION

Derivative Document

June 21, 2003

Change "Subject to Treaty or International Agreement" to 25 years from the date of the source document

Classified By: Joan Smith, Program Analyst
Derived From: [Agency] Memorandum dated May 15, 2000
Declassify On: May 15, 2025

SECRET

THIS DOCUMENT CONTAINS (COUNTRY
OF ORIGIN) INFORMATION

Declassification Instructions on Derivatively Classified Documents:

25X1-human exemption

Source Document

Classified By: Joe Carver, Director
Reason: 1.4(c)
Declassify On: 25X1-human

SECRET

Derivative Document

Classified By: Joan Smith, Program Analyst
Derived From: Department of Good Works Memorandum
   dated June 27, 2010, Subj: (U) Examples
Declassify On: 50X1-HUM

SECRET

"25X1-human" is no longer authorized as a declassification instruction when creating new originally or derivatively classified documents. If your source document contains the "25X1-human" declassification instruction, change it to 50X1-HUM on the newly created derivatively classified document.

Declassification Instructions on Derivatively Classified Documents:

Use of 25X1 through 25X9 Exemptions

The 25X exemptions may only be used on the "Declassify On" line if an agency has identified permanently valuable information that needs to be exempted from automatic declassification at 25 years and has received approval from the Interagency Security Classification Appeals Panel (ISCAP) to exempt the information and to incorporate the exemption into a classification guide. (See 32 CFR Part 2001.26.)

When using an approved exemption, *a date or event that has been approved by the ISCAP must be included with the marking and shall not exceed 50 years from the date of the document.*

 **SECRET**

Department of Good Works
Washington, D.C. 20006

February 15, 2004

MEMORANDUM FOR THE DIRECTOR

From: John E. Doe, Chief Division 5

Subject: (U) Examples

1. (U) Paragraph 1 contains "Unclassified" information. Therefore, this portion will be marked with the designation "U" in parentheses preceding the portion.

2. (S) Paragraph 2 contains "Secret" information. Therefore, this portion will be marked with the designation "S" in parentheses preceding the portion.

Classified By: John E. Doe, Chief Division 5
Derived From: SCG title and date
Declassify On: 25X3, 20540215

SECRET

Derivatively Classifying from a Classification Guide

A classification guide is a document issued by an OCA that provides derivative classification instructions. It describes the elements of information that must be protected, the reason for classification, and the level and duration of classification. The examples on the next page show how to apply instructions from the classification guide to a document.

DEPARTMENT OF GOOD WORKS

Security Classification
Guide No. 129

August 20, 2009

This is a page from a sample guide.

Classification Guide No. 129

Subject	Classification Instructions		
	Level	Reason	Duration
1. Program Planning	U		
2. Program Progress	U		
3. Technical Scope of A.B.C.	C	1.4(e)	25 years see NOTE
4. Vulnerabilities	S	1.4(g)	June 23, 2019
5. Limitations	U		

NOTE: "25 years" denotes 25 years from the date of document creation, not the date of the security classification guide.

September 10, 2009
(U) Title

1. (C) This paragraph includes information about the technical scope of A.B.C.

2. (U) This paragraph includes information on program planning.

3. (U) This paragraph includes information on program progress.

1. Based on guidance from the classification guide, apply appropriate portion markings.

CONFIDENTIAL

September 10, 2009
(U) Title

1. (C) This paragraph includes information about the technical scope of A.B.C.

2. (U) This paragraph includes information on program planning.

3. (U) This paragraph includes information on program progress.

CONFIDENTIAL

2. Apply overall classification markings.

3. Apply classification authority block.

Item 3 in the SCG specifies declassification at 25 years. This is 25 years from the date of document creation.

CONFIDENTIAL
September 10, 2009
(U) Title

1. (C) This paragraph includes information about the technical scope of A.B.C.

2. (U) This paragraph includes information on program planning.

3. (U) This paragraph includes information on program progress.

Classified By: John Doe, Program Analyst
Derived From: Department of Good Works
    Classification Guide No. 129, dated
    August 20, 2009, Item 3
Declassify On: 20340910
CONFIDENTIAL

Classification Extensions

Only an OCA with jurisdiction over the information may extend the duration of classification for <u>up to 25 years</u> from the date of the origin of the document. Any extension beyond 25 years from the date of the origin of the document requires ISCAP approval.

In cases where an extension is made, the "Declassify On" line shall be revised to include the new declassification instructions and shall include the identity of the person authorizing the extension and the date of the action.

Reasonable attempts should be made to notify all holders of a classification extension. As appropriate, classification guides shall be updated to reflect such extensions.

SECRET

Department of Good Works
Washington, D.C. 20006

June 27, 2008

MEMORANDUM FOR THE DIRECTOR

From: John E. Doe, Chief Division 5

Subject: (U) Examples

1. (U) Paragraph 1.

2. (S) Paragraph 2.

Classified By: John E. Doe, Chief Division 5
Reason: 1.4(a)
Declassify On: ~~20151231~~

    Classification extended on August 5, 2010
    until June 27, 2033 by Steven Brown,
    Director, Department of Good Works

SECRET

Classification by Compilation

Section 1.7(e) of E.O. 13526 states that compilations of items of information that are individually unclassified may be classified if the compiled information reveals an additional association or relationship that: (1) meets the standards for classification under this order; and (2) is not otherwise revealed in the individual items of information. The Order also defines compilation as an aggregation of pre-existing unclassified items of information.

For the purpose of marking a document, this means that it may be possible to have a classified document in which all the individual portions are unclassified but because the compilation of the unclassified information reveals an association or relationship not otherwise evident when the portions are used individually, classification of the document and the application of required classification markings are warranted. In these cases, as required by 32 CFR Part 2001.24(g), clear instructions must be provided as to the circumstances under which the individual portions constitute a classified compilation and when they do not.

Two additional crucial points to consider are: (1) as with all other markings, information must be marked in a uniform and conspicuous manner so as to leave no doubt as to the classified status of the information, the level of protection required, the reason for classification, and the duration of classification; and (2) access to or the sharing of unclassified information must not be impeded by unnecessarily or inappropriately applying classification where it's not warranted.

Examples of markings that may be applied to documents that are classified by compilation are on the next page.

Example 1   SECRET

Department of Good Works
Washington, D.C. 20006

June 27, 2008

1. (U) This paragraph, when associated with paragraph 2, is classified SECRET.

2. (U) This paragraph, when associated with paragraph 1, is classified SECRET.

Classified By: John E. Doe, Chief Division 5
Reason: 1.4(a)
Declassify On: 20151231

Classified by compilation: The individual portions of this document are unclassified (and may be used, stored, transmitted, and shared as unclassified) except where otherwise noted within the body of the document.

SECRET

In the first example, guidance is embedded in the individual paragraphs explaining that when the first two paragraphs are associated with one another, the information they reveal is classified. However, note that individually the paragraphs are marked (U), which indicates that when this information stands alone and is not associated with the other paragraph, it is unclassified and may be treated as such. The explanation in bold at the bottom of the document is an example of how to indicate classification by compilation and provide additional guidance to intended recipients.

In the second example, compilation guidance is explained on the bottom of the page, as shown here, or alternatively, is cited in an opening paragraph. Note, as in the first example, that individually the paragraphs are marked (U), which indicates that when this information is standing alone and not associated with the other paragraph, it is unclassified and may be treated as such.

Example 2   SECRET

Department of Good Works
Washington, D.C. 20006

June 27, 2008

1. (U) This paragraph contains the weight of widget A.

2. (U) This paragraph contains the height of widget A.

3. (U) This paragraph contains the length of widget A.

4. (U) This paragraph contains the cost of widget A.

Classified By: John E. Doe, Chief Division 5
Reason: 1.4(a)
Declassify On: 20151231

Classified by compilation: The weight of widget A when combined with or used in association with the height of widget A, is classified Secret. In all other instances the individual portions or combinations of portions of this document are unclassified.

SECRET

Foreign Government Information

Some agencies may require that documents containing classified foreign government information be marked with:

"This document contains (country of origin) information."

Mark the portions that contain the foreign government information to indicate the country of origin and the classification level. Substitute the words "Foreign Government Information" or "FGI" in instances in which the identity of the specific government must be concealed.

If the fact that information is foreign government information must be concealed, the markings described here shall not be used and the document shall be marked as if it were wholly of U.S. origin.

SECRET

 Department of Good Works
Washington, D.C. 20006

February 15, 2010

MEMORANDUM FOR THE DIRECTOR

From: John E. Doe, Chief Division 5

Subject: (U) Examples

1. (C) Paragraph 1 contains classified information from a U.S. source document. Therefore, this portion will be marked with the designation "C" in parentheses.

2. (Country of Origin S) Paragraph 2 contains classified information marked "Secret" by the country of origin. Therefore, this portion will be marked to indicate the country of origin and the level of classification.

Classified By: John E. Doe, Chief Division 5
Derived From: Multiple Sources
Declassify On: 20350215

SECRET

THIS DOCUMENT CONTAINS (COUNTRY OF ORIGIN) INFORMATION

Note on the "Declassify On" line: Foreign government information must be marked with a declassification date of up to 25 years, unless the originating agency has applied for and received approval from the ISCAP to exempt the FGI from declassification at 25 years. Upon receipt of ISCAP approval, the 25X6 or 25X9 exemption markings, as appropriate, may be used in the "Declassify On" line followed by a date that has been approved by the ISCAP.

Classified By: John E. Doe, Chief Division 5
Derived From: Multiple Sources
Declassify On: 25X6, 20500215

SECRET

THIS DOCUMENT CONTAINS (COUNTRY OF ORIGIN) INFORMATION

Section 3: Additional or Special Markings

Commingling of Restricted Data (RD) and Formerly Restricted Data (FRD) with Information Classified under the Order

To the extent practicable, the commingling in the same document of RD or FRD with information classified under the Order should be avoided. When it is not practicable to avoid such commingling, **the marking requirements in the Order and the Directive, as well as the marking requirements in 10 CFR Part 1045,** *Nuclear Classification and Declassification,* **must be followed.**

For commingled documents, the "Declassify On" line shall not include a declassification date or event and shall instead be annotated with "Not Applicable (or N/A) to RD/FRD portions" and "See source list for NSI portions." The source list, as described in 32 CFR Part 2001.22(c)(1)(ii), shall include the declassification instruction for each of the source documents classified under the Order and shall not appear on the front page of the document.

SECRET//RESTRICTED DATA

 Department of Good Works
Washington, D.C. 20006

February 15, 2004

MEMORANDUM FOR THE DIRECTOR

From: John E. Doe, Chief Division 5

Subject: (U) Examples

1. (S) Paragraph 1 contains "Secret" national security information. Therefore, this portion will be marked with the designation "S" in parentheses preceding the portion.

2. (S//RD) Paragraph 2 contains "Secret Restricted Data" information. Therefore, this portion will be marked with the designation "S//RD" in parentheses preceding the portion.

Classified By: John E. Doe, Chief Division 5
Derived From: SCG title and date
Declassify On: Not applicable to RD/FRD portions. See source list for NSI portions.

SECRET//RESTRICTED DATA

Transmittal Document

A transmittal document can consist of anything that accompanies a classified package such as a memorandum or a staff summary sheet.

An unclassified transmittal document shall indicate on its face:
- The highest classification level of any classified information attached or enclosed;
- Instructions such as *"Unclassified when classified enclosure removed"* or *"Upon removal of attachments, this document is [classification level]."*

A classified transmittal document shall contain the same markings as required on all classified documents (i.e., overall classification, portion markings, classification authority block).

Unclassified Transmittal Document

Classified Transmittal Document

SECRET

 Department of Good Works
Washington, D.C. 20006

June 27, 2010

MEMORANDUM FOR THE DIRECTOR

From: John E. Doe, Chief Division 5

Subject: Transmittal Document

This cover letter will accompany a classified package and will be appropriately marked as a transmittal document.

SECRET

This page UNCLASSIFIED when classified enclosure removed

SECRET

 Department of Good Works
Washington, D.C. 20006

June 27, 2010

MEMORANDUM FOR THE DIRECTOR

From: John E. Doe, Chief Division 5

Subject: (U) Transmittal Document

(S) This cover letter will accompany a classified package and will be appropriately marked as a transmittal document.

Classified By: ID #78596
Derived From: Memo dated May 27, 2010
Declassify On: 20200507

SECRET

NOTE: Some agencies may require portion markings on unclassified transmittal documents. Contact your security manager for agency-specific guidance.

(C) This cover letter will accompany a classified package and will be appropriately marked as a transmittal document.

Classified By: ID #78596
Derived From: Memo dated May 27, 2010
Declassify On: 20200507

Downgrade to CONFIDENTIAL when separated from SECRET enclosures.

SECRET

Classified Transmittal Document that Contains Downgrading Instructions

Transmittal Document - E-mails can also serve as transmittal documents.

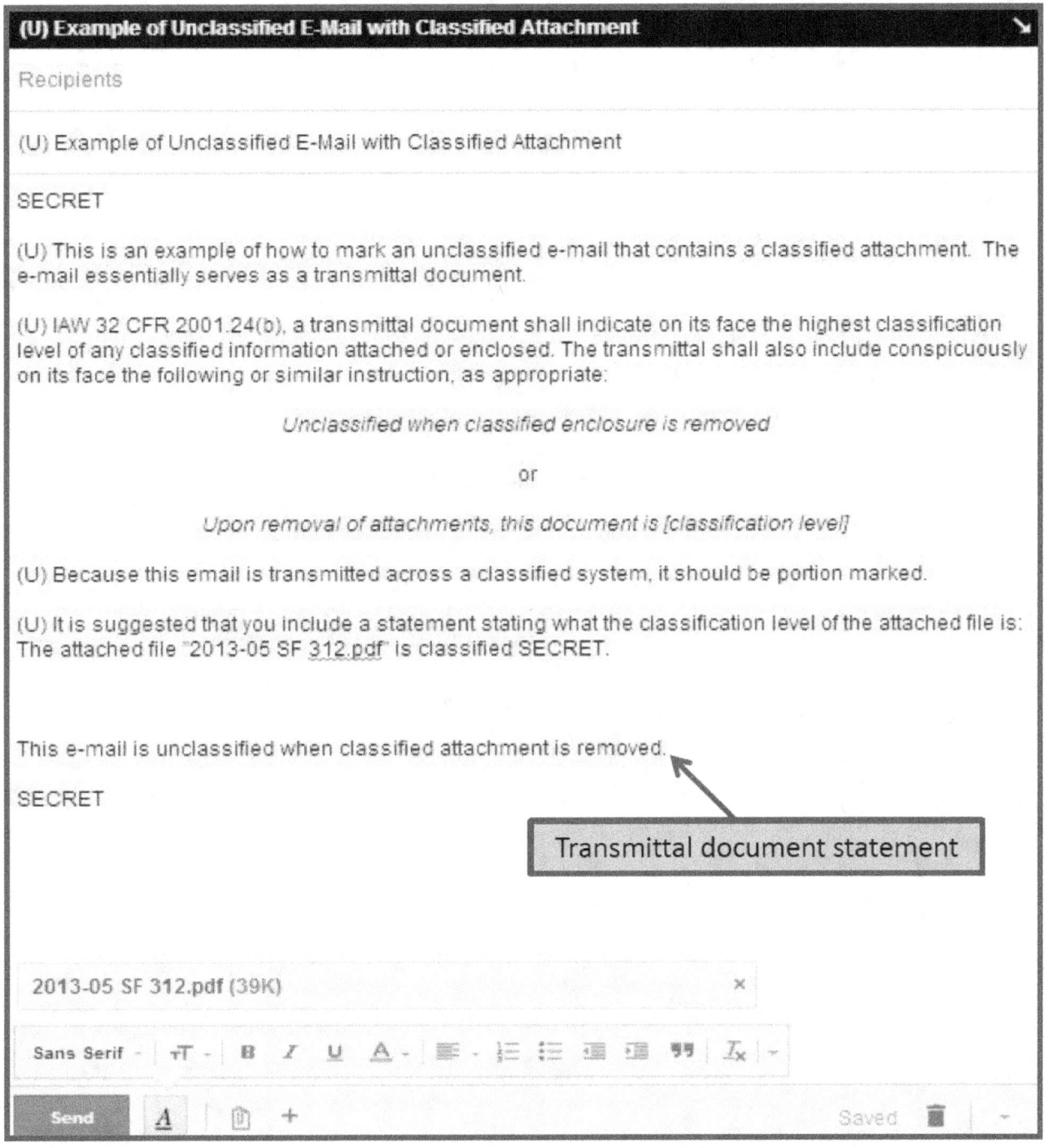

(U) Example of Unclassified E-Mail with Classified Attachment

Recipients

(U) Example of Unclassified E-Mail with Classified Attachment

SECRET

(U) This is an example of how to mark an unclassified e-mail that contains a classified attachment. The e-mail essentially serves as a transmittal document.

(U) IAW 32 CFR 2001.24(b), a transmittal document shall indicate on its face the highest classification level of any classified information attached or enclosed. The transmittal shall also include conspicuously on its face the following or similar instruction, as appropriate:

Unclassified when classified enclosure is removed

or

Upon removal of attachments, this document is [classification level]

(U) Because this email is transmitted across a classified system, it should be portion marked.

(U) It is suggested that you include a statement stating what the classification level of the attached file is: The attached file "2013-05 SF 312.pdf" is classified SECRET.

This e-mail is unclassified when classified attachment is removed.

SECRET

Transmittal document statement

2013-05 SF 312.pdf (39K)   ×

Sans Serif - ͳT - B I U A - ≡ - ≝ ≔ ⇥ ⇤ ❞ Ʇx -

Send   A   🗐   +   Saved 🗑 -

Slide Presentations

SECRET

(U) Examples of PowerPoint Slide Markings

May 27, 2010

Classified By: ID #85967
Derived From: SCG Title, Date
Declassify On: 20150527

SECRET

← **Title slide:**
•Portion markings
•Overall markings
•Classification authority block (may be placed on either first or last slide of presentation)

SECRET

(U) Example of Slide Markings

• (S) This bullet contains "Secret" information. Therefore, this portion will be marked with the designation "S" in parentheses preceding the portion.
• (U) This bullet contains "Unclassified" information. Therefore this portion will be marked with the designation "U" in parentheses preceding the portion.

SECRET

Slide 2:
•Portion markings
•Overall markings

SECRET

(U) This slide demonstrates how to properly mark a slide that contains a chart, graph, picture, etc.

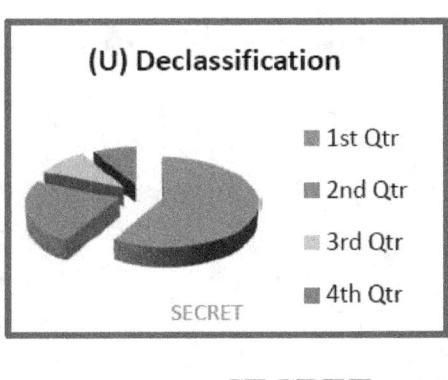

(U) Declassification

■ 1st Qtr
■ 2nd Qtr
■ 3rd Qtr
■ 4th Qtr

SECRET

SECRET

← **Slide 3:**
•Portion markings
•Overall markings

In this example, the portion marking applied to the graphic is spelled out (SECRET) instead of being abbreviated. This is a recommended way to apply markings that provide distinction between the classified status of a graphic, the title of a graphic, and the overall classification of a slide.

2 SECRET

1 (U) Introduction to Marking Slide Presentations

August 17, 2010

3 Classified By: ID #85967
4. Derived From: Multiple Sources
5. Declassify On: 20150817

6. Mutiple Sources: Basic SCG, January 5, 2009
[Agency] Memo, March 10, 2010, Subj: (U) Markings

2 SECRET

1. Portion marking
2. Overall classification of document
3. "Classified by:" line
4. "Derived from:" line
5. "Declassify on:" line
6. List of multiple sources

May be annotated on either first or last slide

SECRET 2.

1 (U) Marking Requirements

1 (U) Topic number 1
1 (U) Topic number 2
1 (U) Topic number 3
1 (U) Topic number 4
1 (U) Topic number 5

SECRET 2.

1. Portion marking
2. Overall classification of page

Note: the overall classification on internal slide may be the classification of the document, or the classification of the individual slide.

UNCLASSIFIED 2.

1. (U) Marking Requirements

1. (U) Topic number 1.
1. (U) Topic number 2.
1. (U) Topic number 3.
1. (U) Topic number 4.
1. (U) Topic number 5.

UNCLASSIFIED 2.

SECRET

(U) Use of Bullet Points

- (S) Main bullet 1
  - Sub-bullet 1
  - Sub-bullet 2
  - Sub-bullet 3

Note: per 32 CFR 2001.21(c)(3), if the sub-portions are the same classification as the main portion, the sub-portions do not require marking.

- (U) Main bullet 2
  - (S) Sub-bullet 1
  - (U) Sub-bullet 2
  - (U) Sub-bullet 3
  - (S) Sub-bullet 4
  - (C) Sub-bullet 5

However, if the portions are not all the same classification, then all main and sub-bullets must be individually marked.

The same rules apply for paragraphs and sub-paragraphs

Classified By: ID # 87596
Derived From: SCG title, dtd 17 April 2009
Declassify On: 20140417

SECRET

SECRET

- (S) Main paragraph 1
  - Sub-paragraph 1
  - Sub-paragraph 2
  - Sub-paragraph 3
- (U) Main paragraph 2
  - (S) Sub-paragraph 1
  - (U) Sub-paragraph 2
  - (U) Sub-paragraph 3
  - (C) Sub-paragraph 4
  - (S) Sub-paragraph 5

Classified By: ID # 87596
Derived From: SCG title, dtd 17 April 2009
Declassify On: 20140417

SECRET

Options for Marking Complex Slides

NOTE: These options are to be used only on complex slides where portion marking everything would be difficult and would detract from the information on the slide itself.

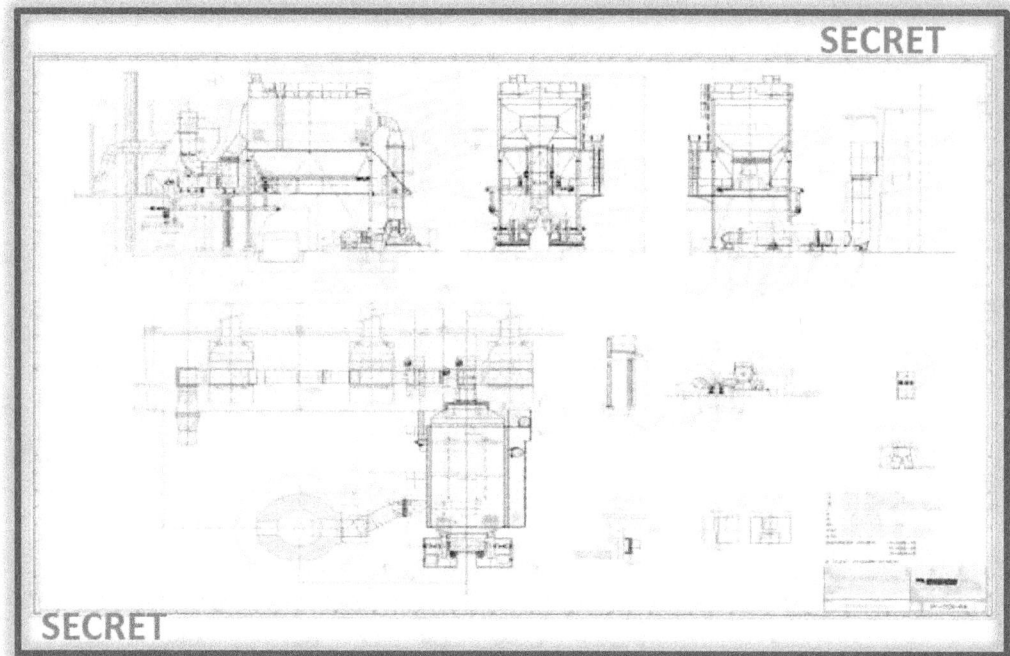

Option 1: When all portions are classified at the same level, mark the overall classification of the slide only; this annotates that everything on this diagram is classified at that level.

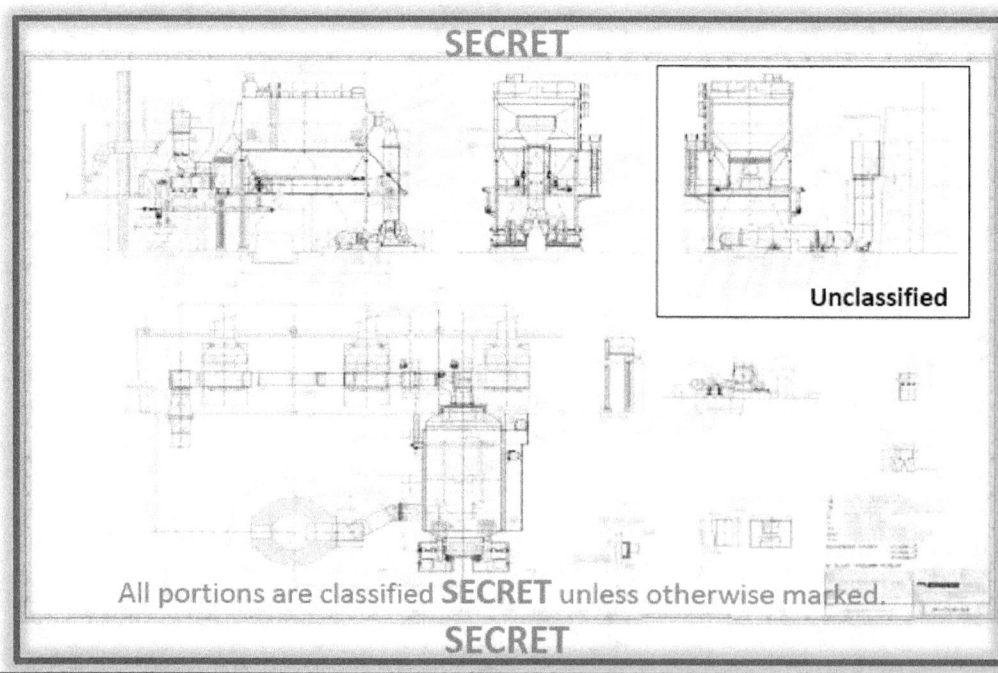

Option 2: When a majority of the portions are classified, mark the overall classification of the slide, indicate the classification of the majority of the portions, and portion mark the exceptions.

> *NOTE: These options are to be used only on complex slides where portion marking everything would be difficult and would detract from the information on the slide itself.*

Option 3: *When a majority of the portions are unclassified, mark the overall classification of the slide, indicate that the majority of the portions are unclassified, and portion mark the classified portions.*

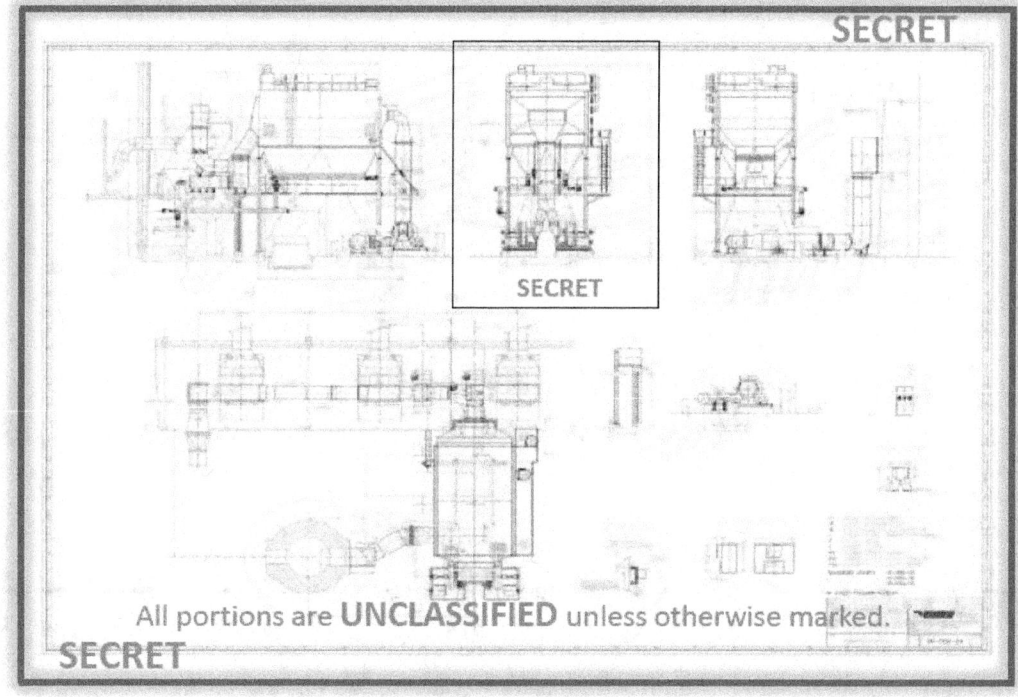

E-Mail

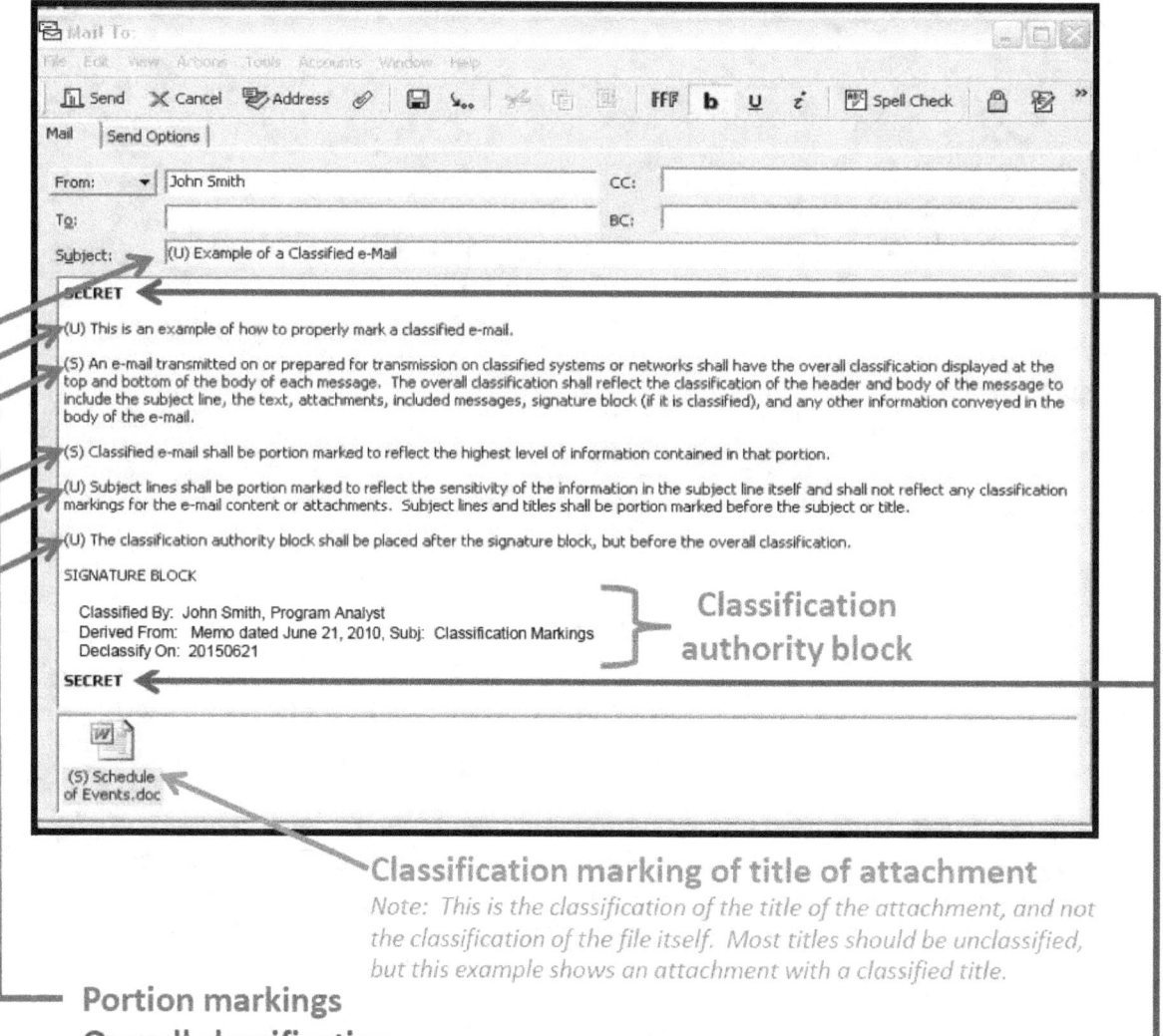

Classification authority block

Classification marking of title of attachment

Note: This is the classification of the title of the attachment, and not the classification of the file itself. Most titles should be unclassified, but this example shows an attachment with a classified title.

Portion markings
Overall classification

Declassified Documents

32 CFR 2001.25 Declassification Markings

(b) The following markings shall be applied to records, or copies of records, regardless of the media:

(1) The word, "Declassified"

(2) The identity of the declassification authority, by name and position, or by personal identifier, **or** the title and date of the declassification guide

(3) The date of declassification

(4) The overall classification markings that appear on the cover page or first page shall be lined with an "X" or straight line.

NOTE: for clarification, the classification markings on **all** pages should be lined through .

Cross out the classified portion markings and remark

Cross out the overall classification markings and remark

Add the authority for the declassification action and the date of declassification

---

DECLASSIFIED ~~SECRET~~

Department of Good Works
Washington, D.C. 20006

June 27, 2010

MEMORANDUM FOR THE DIRECTOR

From: John E. Doe, Chief Division

Subject: (U) Examples

Declassified by: John E. Doe, Chief Division 5
Declassified on: 20130105

1. (U) Paragraph 1 contains "Unclassified" information. Therefore, this portion will be marked with the designation "U" in parentheses preceding the portion.

(U) • (S) If all sub-paragraphs are the same classification as the primary paragraph, then you do not need to portion mark the sub-paragraphs.

 • (U) However, if the portions are not all the same classification, then all main and sub-paragraphs must be individually marked.

(U)
2. (S) Paragraph 2 contains "Secret" information. Therefore, this portion will be marked with the designation "S" in parentheses preceding the portion.

Classified By: John E. Doe, Chief Division 5 or
 ID # 54632
Reason: 1.4(c)
Declassify On: 20300627

 ~~SECRET~~ **DECLASSIFIED**

This only applies to documents that are still in possession of the agency . This is usually seen with documents that are requested under FOIA, MDR, or declassified under the discretionary authority of an agency.

Records that are being reviewed for automatic declassification under section 3.3 of the Order and records accessioned to the National Archives should not be remarked.

Marking of Electronic Storage Media and Equipment

Note: for CDs/DVDs, it may not be advisable to attach a Standard Form label as it may damage the disk drive. However, if you do not use the SF labels, then you must either use a CD label with the appropriate markings on it, or write the classification information on the CD itself.

Label all removable media with the highest classification level of any system into which the media has been inserted.
(Ref: CNSSP-26, para. 5.h)

Label with the highest classification level of information authorized to be processed on the device

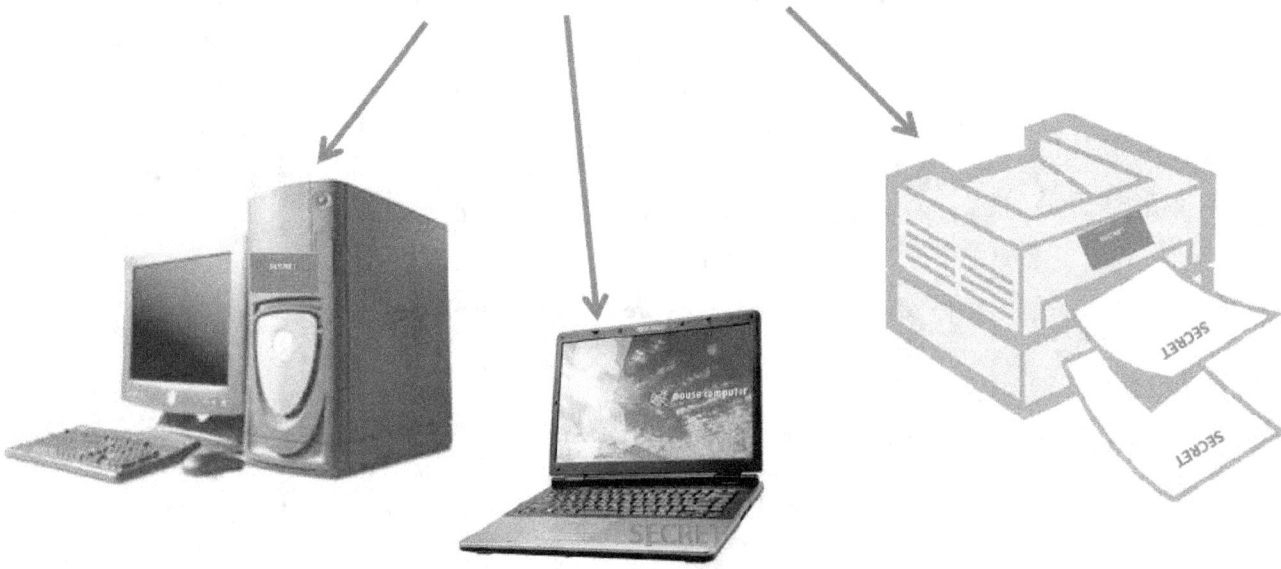

Within a classified environment, the following labels are authorized for use:
(Ref: 32 CFR 2001.80)

SF 706	SF 707	SF 708	SF 709	SF 710
This medium is classified **TOP SECRET** U.S. Government Property. Protect it from unauthorized disclosure in compliance with applicable executive orders, statutes, and regulations.	This medium is classified **SECRET**	This medium is classified **CONFIDENTIAL** U.S. Government Property Protect it from unauthorized disclosure in compliance with applicable executive orders, statutes, and regulations.	This medium is **CLASSIFIED** U.S. Government Property Protect it from unauthorized disclosure in compliance with applicable executive orders, statutes, and regulations.	This medium is **UNCLASSIFIED** U.S. Government Property SF 710 (1-87)

Section 5: Quick Reference

Summary of Classification Authority Block

| Originally Classified Document | Derivatively Classified Document |

Classified By:
Reason:
Declassify On:

Classified By:
Derived From:
Declassify On:

Classified By: the name and position or personal identifier of the creator of the document.

Reason: reason [from E.O. 13526, Section 1.4] information is classified. *Annotated only on originally classified documents.*

Derived From: information identifying the source document. *Annotated only on derivatively classified documents.*

Declassify On: the date the document is to be declassified.

Reasons for Classification E.O. 13526, Section 1.4

(a) military plans, weapons systems, or operations
(b) foreign government information
(c) intelligence activities (including covert action), intelligence sources or methods, or cryptology
(d) foreign relations or foreign activities of the United States, including confidential sources
(e) scientific, technological, or economic matters relating to the national security
(f) United States Government programs for safeguarding nuclear materials or facilities
(g) vulnerabilities or capabilities of systems, installations, infrastructures, projects, plans, or protection services relating to the national security
(h) the development, production, or use of weapons of mass destruction

25X Exemptions from Automatic Declassification E.O. 13526, Section 3.3(b)

Specific information, the release of which should clearly and demonstrably be expected to:

(1) reveal the identify of a confidential human source, a human intelligence source, a relationship with an intelligence or security service of a foreign government or international organization, or a non-human intelligence source; or impair the effectiveness of an intelligence method currently in use, available for use, or under development

(2) reveal information that would assist in the development, production, or use of weapons of mass destruction

(3) reveal information that would impair U.S. cryptologic systems or activities

(4) reveal information that would impair the application of state-of-the-art technology wi U.S. weapon system

(5) reveal formally named or numbered U.S. military war plans that remain in effect, or re operational or tactical elements of prior plans that are contained in such active plans

(6) reveal information, including foreign government information, that would cause serious relations between the United States and a foreign government, or to ongoing diplomatic a of the United States

(7) reveal information that would impair the current ability of United States Government to protect the President, Vice President, and other protectees for whom protection servi the interest of the national security, are authorized

(8) reveal information that would seriously impair current national security emergency preparedness plans or reveal current vulnerabilities of systems, installations, or infrastru relating to the national security

(9) violate a statute, treaty, or international agreement that does not permit the automat unilateral declassification of information at 25 years.

50X Exemptions from Automatic Declassification E.O. 13526, Section 3

(1) the identity of a confidential human source or a human intelligence source (50X1-HUM
(2) key design concepts of weapons of mass destruction (50X2-WMD)
(3) in extraordinary cases, additional specific information formally approved by the ISCA

75X Exemptions from Automatic Declassification E.O. 13526, Section 3.

Specific information that has been formally approved by the ISCAP.

Changed Items

❖Updated references to E.O. 13526, dated December 29, 2009, and 32 CFR Part 2001, dated June 25, 2010.
❖Page 2: updated listing of unauthorized markings.
❖Page 5: portion markings will be placed <u>preceding</u> the portion.
❖Page 7: the original classification authority identified in the "Classified By" line may be by name and position or by personal identifier.
❖Page 15: updated and expanded information for use of "Multiple Sources" on "Derived From" line.
❖Page 34: expanded information on use of transmittal documents.

New Items

❖Page 3: information on use of "50X1-HUM" and "50X2-WMD."
❖Page 9: information on use of "50X1-HUM" and "50X2-WMD."
❖Page 13: guidance on the required identification of derivative classifiers.
❖Guidance for declassification instructions on derivatively classified documents:
    oPage 17: missing declassification instruction on source document.
    oPage 18: "Multiple Sources" on source document.
    oPage 20: "OADR" on source document.
    oPage 21: "X1-X8" exemptions on source document.
    oPage 22: "MR" or "manual review" on source document.
    oPage 23: "DNI Only" or "DCI Only" on source document.
    oPage 24: "Subject to Treaty or International Agreement" on source document.
    oPage 25: "25X1-human" on source document.

❖Page 26: use of "50X" and "75X" exemptions.

❖Page 33: section on "Commingling of Restricted Data (RD) and Formerly Restricted Data (FRD) with Information Classified under the Order."
❖Page 35: examples for slide presentations.
❖Page 40: instructions for marking classified e-mail.
❖Page 41: instructions for marking electronic media.

Revision 1 Changes (January 2012)

❖ Page 2: removed last statement regarding "25X1-human" marking.
❖Page 23: clarified marking requirements for documents marked "DNI Only" or "DCI Only."
❖ Page 25: updated marking requirement for derivative documents when source documents contain "25X1-human."
❖ Page 41: clarified marking policy for removable media.

Revision 2 Changes (January 2014)

❖ Page 2: Reminders, 3rd bullet wording changed to match 32 CFR 2001.24(a). (change marked in purple)
❖ Page 37: new example of e-mail as a transmittal document.
❖ Page 45: added example of declassified document
❖ Page 47: added Section 5: Quick Reference

The Information Security Oversight Office
The National Archives Building
700 Pennsylvania Avenue, NW
Washington, DC 20408

NATIONAL
ARCHIVES